CRAFTY Juggling

Nick Huckleberry Beak

Gareth Stevens Publishing
A WORLD ALMANAC EDUCATION GROUP COMPANY

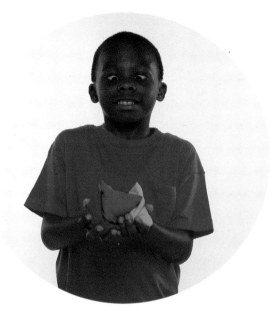

The original publishers would like to thank the following children for modeling for this book: Nichola Barnard, Michael Bewley, Cerys Brunsdon, Alaba Fashina, Fiona Fulton, Camille Kenny-Ryder, Yew Hong Mo, Jessica Moxley, Laurence Ody, Ola Olawe, and Tanyel Yusef. Thanks also to their parents and St. John the Baptist Church of England School.

The author would like to thank Justin from Air Circus and "Smiley Face" from Theatre Crew, Tunbridge Wells, and all those who have put up with his practice over the years. Particular thanks to the Bristol Juggling Convention.

For a free color catalog describing Gareth Stevens' list of high-quality books and multimedia programs, call 1-800-542-2595 (USA) or 1-800-461-9120 (Canada). Gareth Stevens Publishing's Fax: (414) 225-0377.

Library of Congress Cataloging-in-Publication Data

Beak, Nick Huckleberry.
    Crafty juggling / by Nick Huckleberry Beak.
        p. cm. — (Crafty kids)
    Includes bibliographical references and index.
    Summary: Provides instructions on practicing and performing a variety of juggling tricks and directions for making balls and bags to juggle.
        ISBN 0-8368-2502-0 (lib. bdg.)
    1. Juggling—Juvenile literature. [1. Juggling.] I. Beak, Nick Huckleberry. Juggling fun. II. Title. III. Series.
GV1558.B42   2000
793.8'7—dc21   99-41545

This North American edition first published in 2000 by
Gareth Stevens Publishing
A World Almanac Education Group Company
1555 North RiverCenter Drive, Suite 201
Milwaukee, WI 53212 USA

Original edition © 1996 by Anness Publishing Limited. First published in 1996 by Lorenz Books, an imprint of Anness Publishing Limited, New York, New York. This U.S. edition © 2000 by Gareth Stevens, Inc. Additional end matter © 2000 by Gareth Stevens, Inc.

Senior Editor: Caroline Beattie
Photographer: John Freeman
Designer: Edward Kinsey
Gareth Stevens series editor: Dorothy L. Gibbs
Editorial assistant: Diane Laska-Swanke

Printed in Mexico

1 2 3 4 5 6 7 8 9 04 03 02 01 00

Introduction

So — you want to throw things around, do you? Be careful! Juggling is catching, and, once you have read this book, there will be no turning back.

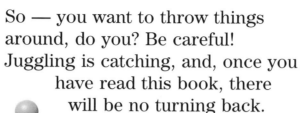

You will start with balls and beanbags. Then you will want to juggle fruits and vegetables. Next it will be plates and cups — or even furniture! OK, maybe furniture is getting a little carried away, but, truly, almost anything can be juggled.

This book shows you how to juggle bean-bags, coins, rope, string, and, believe it or not, cookies and coat hangers! Some of the tricks will take a lot of practice, but others you will be able to do right away. Whether you do them well or not, remember that juggling is about having fun, trying new tricks, and entertaining others. So grab your hat — and juggle it!

Nick Huckleberry Beak

Contents

Things to Juggle

You probably have things around the house you can start juggling with right away, such as an old tennis ball, an apple or an orange, or maybe an old sock filled with rice. Do not try to juggle your mom's favorite dinner plates or your dad's new camera — just yet. You can, of course, buy specially designed juggling equipment, but it really is not necessary, and it is certainly more expensive.

This book includes instructions for making your own juggling balls and beanbags, but, if you look around, you will find many other items to juggle. You can use hats, scarves, and books, or even clothes or shoes. You can, in fact, juggle anything that is not too large, heavy, breakable, or dangerous.

An advantage of juggling unusual items is they often are more entertaining, but... it is not *what* you juggle, it is *how* you juggle it.

Although juggling is fun to watch for a while, it can get boring. So, make your juggling interesting. Tell a joke, wear colorful clothes, make funny noises or a funny face. You will be surprised at how little you have to do to get people laughing and clapping.

Do quick tricks between longer tricks, to keep your audience guessing what you will do next. And, remember, even the same trick done over and over will still be entertaining if you throw the ball higher, lower, faster, or slower each time.

Are you ready? Then get out there and juggle!

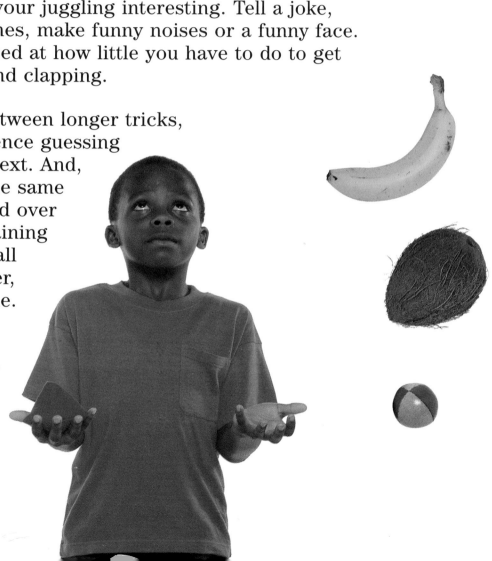

Making a Balloon Ball

Balloon balls are inexpensive, easy to make, and very colorful to juggle.

1 Cut the stems off of two balloons. You will need only the round top part of each balloon.

2 Fill a plastic bag with rice and insert the bag into one of the balloon tops.

YOU WILL NEED
- Four or five balloons (in different colors)
- Scissors
- Small plastic bag
- Rice (uncooked)

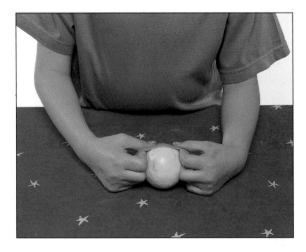

HANDY HINT
Be sure to use good-quality balloons. Cheaper ones tend to split easily and often do not stretch very well, so your juggling balls end up being too small.

3 Place the second balloon over the bag of rice, making sure it covers the open end of the first balloon. The open end of the second balloon does not matter because the first balloon shows through it, creating a nice two-color effect.

4 Cut the stem off of another balloon and cut little pieces out of the round top part of the balloon. When you stretch this balloon over the ball, the colors of the balloons underneath will show through the cutouts.

5 Depending on how many colors you want and how fancy you would like your juggling ball to be, repeat step 4, adding a fourth or even a fifth balloon.

9

Making a Beanbag

YOU WILL NEED

- Scissors
- Cardboard
- Cotton fabric
- Needle
- Thread
- Small plastic bag
- Rice (uncooked)

HANDY HINT

Cotton fabric is best for beanbags because it tends to last longer than many other materials. To fill your beanbag, however, try using dried beans, lentils, millet, corn, or whatever you have in the cupboard at home, instead of rice. Each of these dried foods gives the beanbag a different feel.

1 Cut a 4-inch (10-centimeter) square out of cardboard. Using the cardboard square as a guide, cut out two squares of cotton fabric.

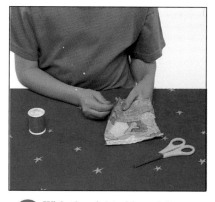

2 With the right sides of the fabric squares facing each other, sew the squares together along three edges to form a kind of pocket or a small fabric bag.

3 Turn the fabric pocket right side out. Then fill a plastic bag with rice and put the bag inside the pocket.

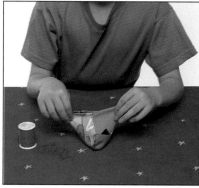

4 Pinch together the fabric at the opening of the pocket to form a pyramid and sew it closed. You are ready to start juggling!

HANDY HINT
Using beanbags that are different colors or have different designs makes it easier to follow each one through the stages of a trick.

Warming Up

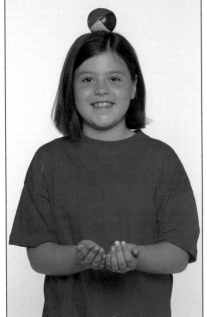

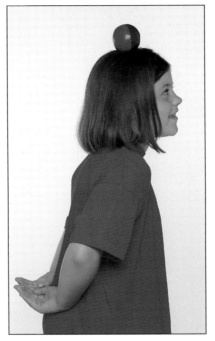

1 Start juggling with some simple warm-ups. First, place a juggling ball on top of your head. Then nod your head and see if you can catch the ball in your hands.

2 Place the juggling ball on your head again. This time, tilt your head backward and catch the ball in your hands behind your back. Hold your hands away from your body a little because the ball will not roll straight down your back.

3 You have probably seen this trick done with a coin. Bend your arm at the elbow and put a juggling ball on your elbow. Let the ball roll off and fall toward the floor.

4 As the ball begins to drop, quickly straighten your arm and catch the ball before it hits the floor. Your hand should be facing palm down (as shown).

5 If you drop a juggling ball, there are ways to pick it up without bending down. Roll the ball with one foot onto the top of your other foot. Then flip the ball up and catch it.

6 To look more stylish, hold the ball between your heels, then jump with both legs, in a backward kick, throwing the ball up so you can catch it.

13

One-Ball Workout

1 To learn juggling, start nice and easy. Hold a juggling ball in your right hand.

2 Throw the ball up, just higher than your head, and, while the ball is in the air, clap your hands. Always keep your eyes on the ball.

3 Catch the ball with your left hand. Try this trick again, clapping your hands three times before you catch the ball.

4 Lift one of your legs, bending it at the knee, and throw the ball up from under that leg. You should still try to clap before you catch the ball.

5 Hold the ball in your right hand, behind your back. Throw the ball up over your left shoulder and catch it in front of you with your left hand. Can you put in a clap, too?

6 This trick will test your balance and might make you a little dizzy. Throw the ball up with your right hand and spin around.

HANDY HINT

To make these tricks a little more difficult, try adding more claps. You could also try to clap underneath your leg and behind your back before you catch the ball.

7 After spinning around once, catch the ball with your left hand. Now try spinning around twice before you catch the ball.

15

Monkey Juggling

Although you will not actually be juggling monkeys, you might look like a monkey when you do this trick. Anyone can do Monkey Juggling, but, to make it work well, you have to be a little silly.

HANDY HINT

To get your audience laughing, bend your arms at the elbows and swing them like a monkey as you place the beanbags under your arms. You can add a few monkey noises, facial expressions, and a monkey walk, too.

1 Place a beanbag (or a banana) under each arm and hold another one in your left hand. Cup your right hand, ready to catch the beanbag that you will drop from under your right arm.

2 After catching the beanbag in your right hand, place the one in your left hand under your right arm. Straighten your left arm, ready to catch the beanbag that will drop from under your left arm.

3 As you catch the beanbag in your left hand, place the one in your right hand under your left arm. Straighten your right arm and catch the right beanbag again.

4 As you continue to repeat the pattern, try to speed up your movements. While you're at it, why not make some jungle noises?

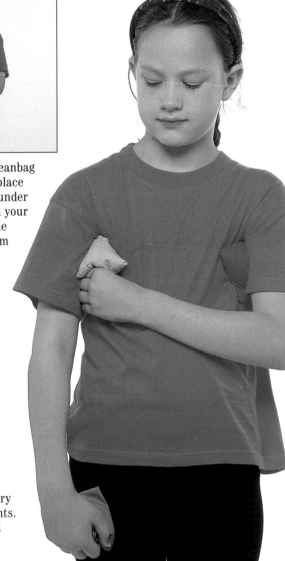

17

Two-Ball Juggle

1 Learning to juggle with two balls is easy. First, throw both balls into the air at the same time, in straight lines. Then catch them.

2 Now throw both balls up at the same time so they cross in midair. Catch them in the opposite hands. Do not let the balls collide!

3 Throw both balls straight up again, at the same time. Then cross your arms in front of you and catch the balls in the opposite hands.

4 Relax and do this trick slowly. If you learn this one well, you will be ready to juggle three balls. Hold a juggling ball in each hand.

5 Throw the right-hand ball diagonally to the left. Keep your eyes on the ball. Just as the ball is about to drop, throw the left-hand ball diagonally to the right.

6 As you catch the right-hand ball in your left hand, keep looking at the left-hand ball, which is still in the air.

HANDY HINT

To make these tricks more difficult, try clapping before you catch the balls. Two-ball juggling is good practice before you really start to juggle.

7 Now catch the left-hand ball in your right hand. Smile — you did it!

Juggler's Nightmare

This trick is not scary;
it is just difficult to do.
Challenge your friends!

1 With your arms crossed near
the wrists, hold a juggling ball
in each hand. You will find it hard to
keep your arms crossed when you
throw the balls, but pushing your
arms against each other will help
keep you from uncrossing them.

2 Throw both balls up at the same time so they will cross each other and land in the opposite hands. Remember to keep your arms crossed! You will have to throw one ball higher than the other so the balls do not collide in midair.

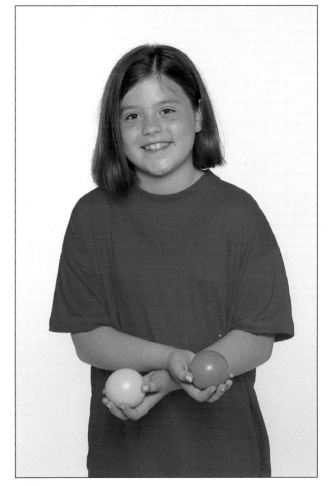

3 Catch both balls. If your hands are still crossed, well done. If not, try again. Getting the hang of this trick will take some practice.

One Hand Only

1 Hold two balls in one hand. Holding them side by side is usually best, but do what is most comfortable for you. Start by throwing the balls straight up, side by side.

2 Throw the first ball, then move your hand to one side to throw the second ball, so it will not collide with the first ball coming down.

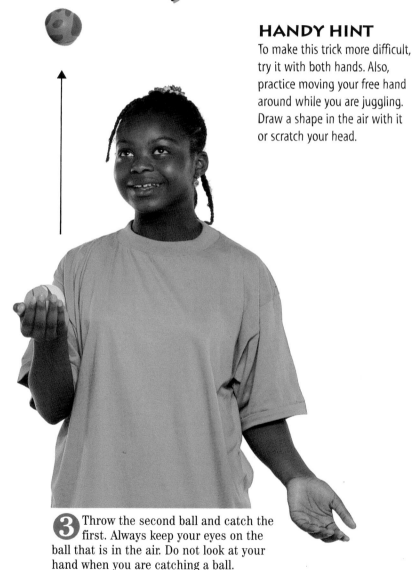

HANDY HINT
To make this trick more difficult, try it with both hands. Also, practice moving your free hand around while you are juggling. Draw a shape in the air with it or scratch your head.

3 Throw the second ball and catch the first. Always keep your eyes on the ball that is in the air. Do not look at your hand when you are catching a ball.

4 Instead of throwing the balls up side by side, try throwing them in a clockwise or a counter-clockwise circle.

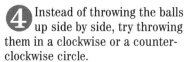

HANDY HINT

Move only your hand. Keep your body still. You will probably find throwing in one direction easier than the other.

Ups and Downs

1 If you practiced the last trick, you should be ready for this one. Hold three beanbags — two in your right hand and one in your left.

2 Throw a beanbag straight up from each hand, trying to get them both to the same height. Be ready to throw the third beanbag straight up between them, just as they start to come down.

3 After throwing the third beanbag, catch the first two, but keep your eyes on the one in the air. Be ready to throw the first two beanbags again, when the third starts to come down.

④ Keep repeating this trick as long as possible.

HANDY HINT

To make Ups and Downs look more impressive, throw the beanbags so they cross each other, instead of moving up and down in straight lines.

The Yo-Yo Juggle

1 This trick is not very easy, but it is very funny to watch. You imagine that two juggling balls are joined by a thread, so you must try to keep the balls the same distance apart when you are juggling them.

2 To make it look as if you are lifting the lower ball with the upper ball, raise the ball you are holding in your upper hand while, at the same time, gently throwing the lower ball upward.

3 Pretend to tie a thread to only one of the balls. Hold your free hand up as if you were holding the thread tight.

4 When you lift your upper hand, throw the "threaded" ball. Be sure to keep the same distance between your hand and the ball.

HANDY HINT

Before starting this trick, let the audience see you pretending to tie the balls together with a thin thread. You might actually fool some of them!

5 As the "threaded" ball starts to come down, throw up the other ball, leaving a hand free to catch the "threaded" ball.

HANDY HINT

With practice, the Yo-Yo Juggle can look very convincing. If you really want to impress people, use three balls instead of two. Hold the third ball in your upper hand. It should appear to be tied to one of the lower balls.

Coin and Card Capers

1 This trick is not as difficult as it looks. Extend your index finger and carefully balance a playing card on it.

2 Then, hold a coin by its edges and place it on the card, directly over the tip of the finger below it. A heavy coin, such as a quarter, works best.

3 Now, gently grasp one corner of the card. Keep your hands steady and get ready to pull the card away.

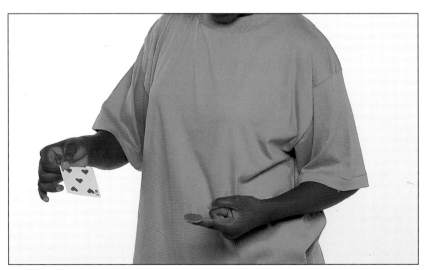

4 Pull the card very quickly, trying not to lift it up or push it down. With a steady hand and a little luck, the coin will be sitting on the tip of your index finger.

28

1 If you really feel lucky, set up the card and the coin as before. Instead of pulling the card, however, you will flick it away with your finger.

2 Ready? Flick the card quickly. You will amaze yourself as well as your friends.

HANDY HINT
You must keep the card horizontal when you pull it away. It is easy to pull it up or push it down by being too enthusiastic.

Three-Ball Frenzy

1 Grab three balls. It is time for your first real juggle. Hold two of the balls in the hand with which you will throw first. Hold the third ball in the other hand.

2 Now follow the pictures. Throw the yellow ball up diagonally. When the yellow ball starts to come down, throw the blue ball. Catch the yellow ball in your free hand.

3 As you catch the yellow ball, keep your eyes on the blue ball in the air. When the blue ball starts to come down, throw the red ball up diagonally.

4 Catch the blue ball in your free hand but keep looking at the red ball. Although it is tempting, try not to look at your hands when you are catching the balls.

HANDY HINT

Count when you juggle, but, instead of counting each throw (one, two, three, four), count one, one, one, one, etc. Although it sounds strange, it will help you slow down, which makes juggling a little easier.

5 Finally, catch the red ball in the hand that is holding the yellow ball. You have just completed your first juggle. Do it again! As you practice, remember to throw the balls sideways, rather than forward.

Flashy Starts

1 Now that you can juggle, you have to make it fun to watch. So here is a flashy way to start. Hold two balls in one hand and one ball in the other.

2 Throw two balls, one from each hand, straight up at the same time (see page 18). When these two balls start coming down, throw the third ball up diagonally.

3 Catch the first two balls, one in each hand, but keep your eyes on the ball in the air. As it comes down, start doing a normal juggling sequence.

1 This flashy start is another favorite. Although it looks very difficult, it is really easy. Begin with the hand holding two balls facing down toward the floor. Then, very quickly, turn that hand, so it is facing up, and throw the balls into the air.

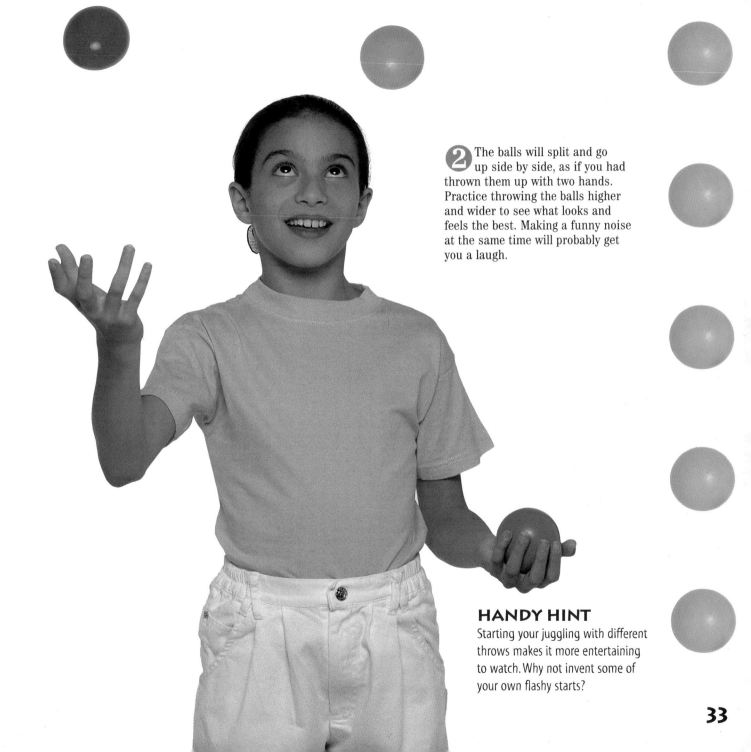

2 The balls will split and go up side by side, as if you had thrown them up with two hands. Practice throwing the balls higher and wider to see what looks and feels the best. Making a funny noise at the same time will probably get you a laugh.

HANDY HINT
Starting your juggling with different throws makes it more entertaining to watch. Why not invent some of your own flashy starts?

Mighty Muscles

This trick might sound and look pretty silly, but it is easy to do and can be very funny if it is done well. Don't worry! You do not need big muscles to do it.

1 Hold three beanbags, as though you are about to begin juggling, and tell your audience that you are going to do the Mighty Muscles juggle.

2 Throw one beanbag from your right hand into the air, either straight up or diagonally. Try to throw it a little higher than you normally would.

3 Keeping your eyes on the beanbag in the air, bend your right arm and put the beanbag you are holding in your left hand into the bend of your right elbow.

4 Catch the falling beanbag in your left hand. Then flex your right arm and point to it with your left hand to pretend you are showing off your enormous biceps.

HANDY HINT

Really exaggerate your movements and expressions — this trick was meant to be silly. To make it even sillier, let the beanbag fall off your arm, but pretend not to notice. You will still be grinning and pointing but, now, at nothing. After a while, notice that the beanbag is gone and look shocked. The audience will probably have been trying to tell you about it for some time!

Under or Over

1 This trick will show you how to juggle under your legs! To make balancing easier, always lift up your leg, rather than bend down to it. Start with two balls in your right hand and one in your left hand.

2 Throw one of the balls in your right hand up diagonally to the left from under your right leg. Your right arm should go under your leg so the ball can travel up, not just to the side. Keep your eyes on the ball in the air.

3 Throw the ball you are holding in your left hand so you can catch the first ball in that hand. Now you are back to a normal juggling pattern.

4 Catch the second ball in your right hand and keep juggling normally. Then throw a ball under your leg and try to keep going. With practice, you will get better.

1 Try some more body twisting. Hold two balls in your right hand, behind your back, and turn your head to look over your left shoulder. Keep your body relaxed.

2 Throw one ball from your right hand straight up so it travels over your left shoulder. Bring your right hand back to its normal position in front of you.

3 Throw the ball you are holding in your left hand so you can catch the first ball coming down. Then catch the second ball in your right hand.

4 Start juggling normally, then see if you can quickly throw a ball over your shoulder and keep juggling. This trick is a good practice exercise.

Cookie Juggling

Challenge your friends to try this trick and watch the funny faces they make. How many people can say they have juggled cookies — without using their hands or feet?

HANDY HINT

If you wear glasses, be sure you take them off before you try this trick!

38

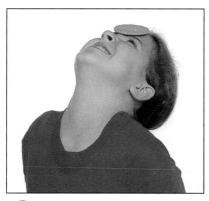

1 Tilt your head back and place a cookie on your forehead. Use a cookie that is not too crumbly so you will not get crumbs in your eyes.

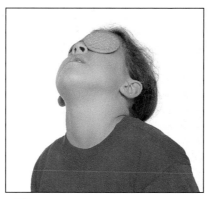

2 Try to move the cookie down to your mouth by making faces and wriggling your facial muscles. Keep your head tilted backward.

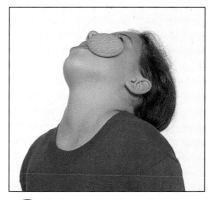

3 Try to move the cookie down onto one cheek. (Moving it along your nose will cause trouble.) Now tilt your head to one side.

4 Use your tongue to pull the cookie into your mouth. Then, take a bow and enjoy the applause — or just eat the cookie!

Body Bouncing

1 These tricks are fun to do in the middle of a juggling routine. Start by throwing one ball into the air. As the ball comes down, bounce it off some part of your body.

2 Turn your hand palm down and bounce the ball off the back of it. Try to bounce the ball straight up. Sometimes it will bounce at funny angles, making it harder to catch.

3 Extend your arm and bounce the ball off your forearm. This trick is very easy. You could even catch the ball on your forearm and throw it up again.

HANDY HINT

You do not have to do these tricks one after the other. Just try one every now and then to make your juggling more exciting to watch. Of course, if you can do all of them, one after the other, you will probably get a huge round of applause.

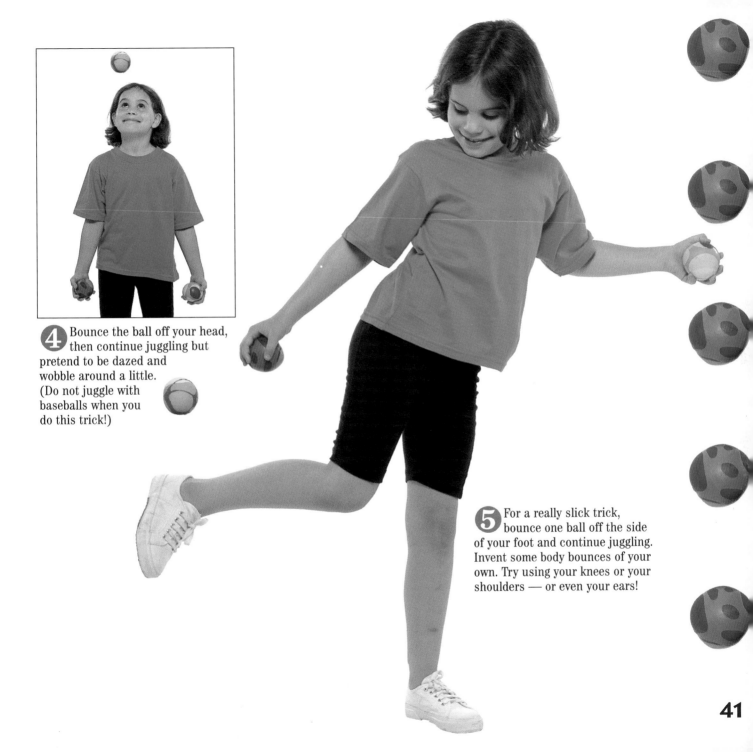

4 Bounce the ball off your head, then continue juggling but pretend to be dazed and wobble around a little. (Do not juggle with baseballs when you do this trick!)

5 For a really slick trick, bounce one ball off the side of your foot and continue juggling. Invent some body bounces of your own. Try using your knees or your shoulders — or even your ears!

41

Juggling Magic

What makes this trick so magical? Well, if you do it with the back of your hand facing the audience, the ball in your hand will be hidden. When you quickly exchange balls, it looks as if a ball has changed color in midair. If you have any doubts, give the trick a try. It will take some practice, however, to get it right.

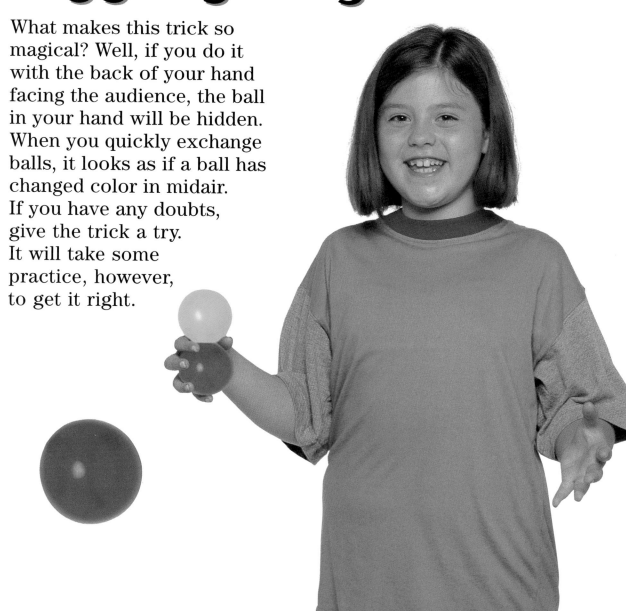

1 Close your hand around one juggling ball and rest another ball on top of it where your thumb and index finger form a C shape.

2 Carefully throw both balls into the air. Your hand should follow them upward. The balls should not go very far and should stay close together, one under the other.

3 Grab the top ball with your hand. When you grab the ball quickly, it feels as though your hand simply slides up to the ball.

4 Quickly move the hand holding the ball underneath the ball in the air. As that ball comes down, catch it on top of your hand, as before (in the C shape formed by your thumb and index finger). To do this trick well, you must move quickly. These moves should be finished before you can say "juggling magic!"

The Coat Hanger Swing

1 Pull a wire coat hanger into a diamond shape (as shown). This coat hanger is covered with colored tape to make it look more like a juggling prop.

2 Hang the coat hanger upside down on your index finger and carefully balance a small coin on the upturned hook at the bottom. You might have to bend the hook a little if it is not facing upward.

3 Start swinging the hanger slowly from side to side. Then swing it around and around in a full circle. The coin should stay on the hanger, but it might fly off, so keep your eyes on it.

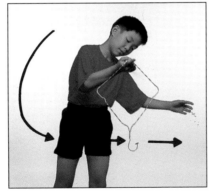

4 Make your last circle swing larger than the others and follow through, keeping the hanger level until it stops swinging. The coin should remain in place. To prove the coin is not stuck on, gently tap the hanger. The coin will fall off.

5 If you feel really adventurous, swing the hanger from a shoelace, instead of your finger. The trick will look more spectacular, although it will actually seem easier. Good luck! You will need it.

Use Your Head

1 Start with a beanbag on your head and one in each hand. Throw the beanbag that you are holding in your right hand.

2 As soon as you have thrown the beanbag, reach up with your right hand and grab the beanbag on top of your head. Keep your eyes on the beanbag in the air.

3 Throw the beanbag you are holding in your left hand so you can catch the first beanbag in that hand. At this point, start juggling normally.

4 Throw the beanbag in your right hand and catch the one coming down.

5 Throw the beanbag in your left hand and catch the one coming down.

6 Finally, throw the beanbag in your right hand to catch the one coming down, and put the beanbag in your left hand on top of your head.

Although this trick has a long description, it does not take very long to do. Try it again but, this time, start with the beanbag in your left hand.

7 When you catch the last beanbag in your left hand, you should be back where you began, with a beanbag on your head and one in each hand.

Crazy Juggling

1 Announce that you are going to do an impression of the world's worst baseball team, then quickly throw several beanbags into the air as if you are going to juggle them.

2 Open both hands wide and wave your arms as if you are trying to catch the beanbags, but just let them all drop.

3 When all the beanbags are on the ground, make a desperate face and pretend to be upset. If you are a good actor, this trick will be very funny.

HANDY HINT

These are just some extra tricks that you can sneak into your juggling performance for a little variety. They might not get a huge laugh, but they should get a few chuckles.

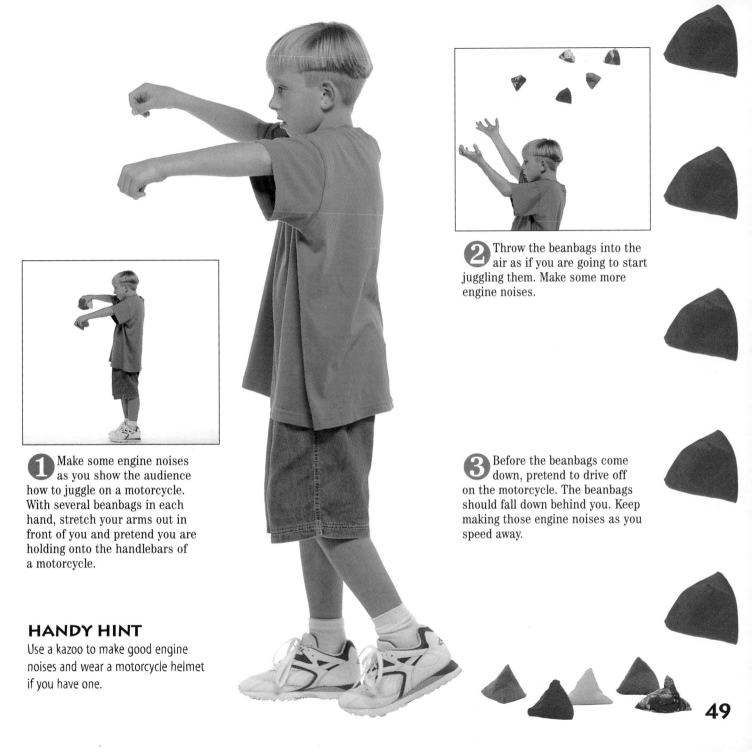

1 Make some engine noises as you show the audience how to juggle on a motorcycle. With several beanbags in each hand, stretch your arms out in front of you and pretend you are holding onto the handlebars of a motorcycle.

HANDY HINT

Use a kazoo to make good engine noises and wear a motorcycle helmet if you have one.

2 Throw the beanbags into the air as if you are going to start juggling them. Make some more engine noises.

3 Before the beanbags come down, pretend to drive off on the motorcycle. The beanbags should fall down behind you. Keep making those engine noises as you speed away.

49

What a Mouthful!

1 Start with a ball in your mouth, a ball in your right hand, and an apple in your left hand. You will throw the ball in your right hand first.

2 As soon as your right hand is empty, grab the ball from your mouth and put your right hand back in position so you will be ready to juggle.

3 Throw the apple you are holding in your left hand so you can catch the first ball in that hand. Be sure to keep your eyes on the apple in the air.

4 Throw the ball you are holding in your right hand and catch the apple in that hand. Move your right hand toward your mouth. Remember to keep your eyes on the ball in the air.

HANDY HINT

You can do this trick with another kind of fruit or with a bun or some other large, soft kind of food. Always be careful when you put anything in your mouth. You do not want to hurt your mouth or damage your teeth!

5 As you put the apple in your mouth with your right hand, throw the ball you are holding in your left hand and catch the ball coming down in that hand. Finally, catch the last ball in your right hand.

Juggling on a String

1 Tie a long piece of string around a juggling ball. Make sure the string is tied tightly so the ball will not pop off when you throw it.

2 Tie the other end of the string around your waist or loop it around a button on your shirt or jacket. Do whatever feels the most comfortable for you.

3 Now get two more juggling balls and stand in a position to start juggling. Hold the ball with the string at the front of your right hand. You will throw this ball first.

4 Stand with your feet apart and throw the ball out in front of you. It will stop as the string pulls tight, then fly backward between your legs.

5 The ball will swing up toward your back, then to the front. Pushing your hips forward will help the ball swing high enough to catch.

6 Catch the ball in your right hand before it swings backward again. Now try this trick while you are juggling the other two balls.

7 If the ball does not swing very well, you might have to adjust the length of the string. The best length depends on your height, so try different lengths to get the best result.

HANDY HINT

This trick always catches people by surprise, but, to add even more surprise, try using clear, lightweight fishing line, instead of string. Unless they are very close to you, people in the audience will not be able to see the fishing line. Also, keep in mind that you can still juggle normally, even with the string attached, as long as you do not throw the ball on the string too high. So, you can start juggling normally, then, suddenly, throw the ball with the string out toward the audience. You can be sure of getting a response!

Over the Top

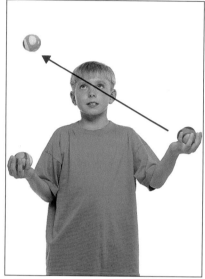

1 Instead of juggling straight across your body, this trick adds a slight change. Throw the first ball from your right hand in an arc over your head. You will have to swing your arm a little more to get the right effect.

2 Now throw the ball in your left hand normally across your body and catch the first ball in your left hand. Not throwing the same way with both hands will probably feel strange.

3 Throw the second ball from your right hand in an arc, then catch the ball thrown from your left hand in your right hand. As you continue this juggling sequence, it almost looks like you are juggling in a circle.

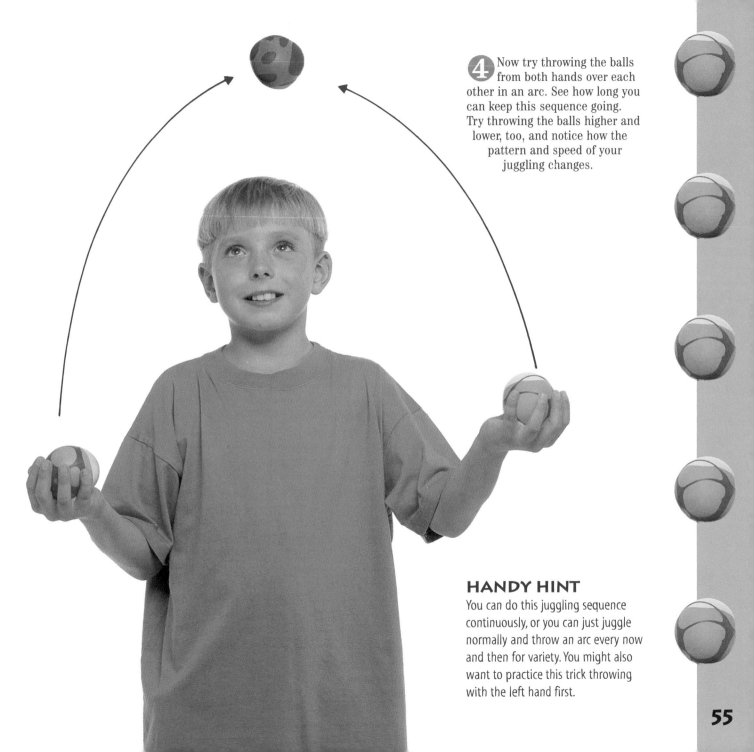

4 Now try throwing the balls from both hands over each other in an arc. See how long you can keep this sequence going. Try throwing the balls higher and lower, too, and notice how the pattern and speed of your juggling changes.

HANDY HINT

You can do this juggling sequence continuously, or you can just juggle normally and throw an arc every now and then for variety. You might also want to practice this trick throwing with the left hand first.

Juggling a Knot

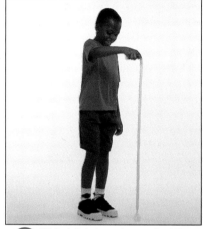

1 This trick is not easy, but it is definitely worth trying. All you need is a piece of soft rope. Any kind of rope, or even string, will do, as long as it is fairly flexible.

2 Pull the rope up sharply and extend the index finger of the hand with which you are holding the rope. The rope will fold over in midair.

3 Hit the rope with your index finger, sideways and slightly downward, but do not hit too near the end of the rope.

4 The rope will swing around and fold over on itself. Because these stages all happen so quickly, you will not actually see them. You will see only the end result.

5 As the rope comes down again, a knot will appear — like magic!

HANDY HINT

When you do this trick for an audience, do not extend your index finger until you are just about to hit the rope with it. You do not want the audience to figure out how the trick is done!

57

Coin, Shirt, and Shoe

1 To make a T-shirt easier to juggle, tie it in a big, loose knot. Tying the shirt keeps it from flapping around when you throw it.

2 You will also need a coin and a shoe for this trick. The heavier the coin is, the easier it will be to juggle.

3 To start this juggling sequence, it is probably best to throw the coin first, but you could choose something else. This juggle is not as easy as it looks because the items you will be juggling have such different weights and shapes. Time yourself to see how long you can keep the sequence going.

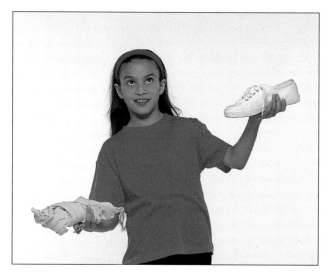

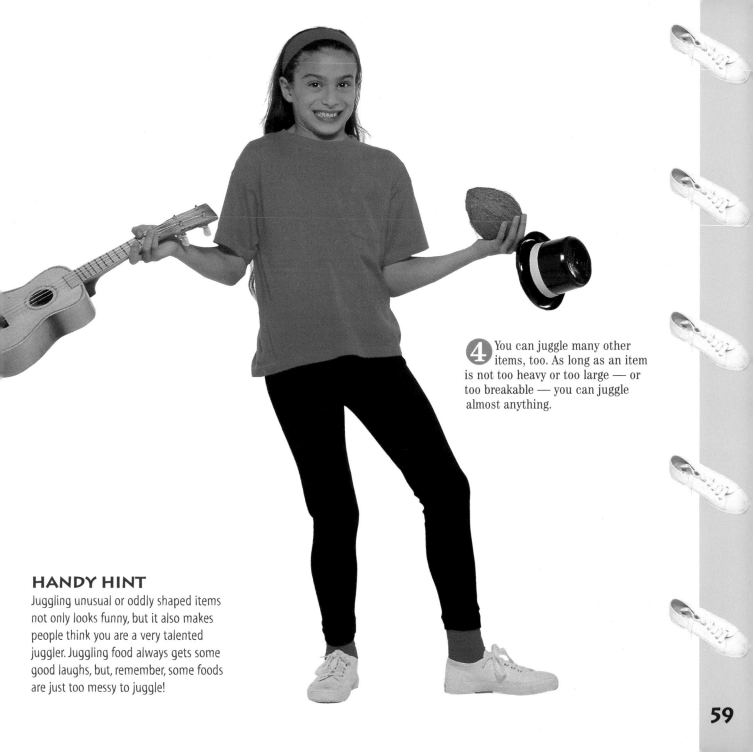

4 You can juggle many other items, too. As long as an item is not too heavy or too large — or too breakable — you can juggle almost anything.

HANDY HINT

Juggling unusual or oddly shaped items not only looks funny, but it also makes people think you are a very talented juggler. Juggling food always gets some good laughs, but, remember, some foods are just too messy to juggle!

Hat-on-Head Finale

1 Choose a hat that fits loosely on your head. A hat with a stiff brim works best. Hold the back brim of the hat with both hands.

2 Then throw the hat up so it starts turning over in the air. Practice throwing the hat so it does not turn too much or too little.

3 Finally, let the hat drop onto your head and spread your arms to signal the audience that you are ready for applause.

1 You can also use your hat for a final juggling trick that will add a little extra flourish to the end of your routine.

2 Throw the balls you have been juggling into the air. Try to keep the balls closely grouped.

3 Keeping your eyes on the balls in the air, quickly grab your hat with both hands and take it off your head.

4 Turn the hat over and catch the balls in it. Remember to take the balls out of the hat before you put it back on your head.

HANDY HINT

There are lots of ways to juggle a hat. Try throwing it with one hand, or off your foot, onto your head. Then think up some other challenges on your own.

Glossary

arc: (n) a line or path that curves to form part of a circle or an arch.

biceps: a large muscle located at the front of a person's upper arm.

challenge: (v) to call on or dare a person, sometimes as a contest, to show skill or effort, or to take on a difficult task.

collide: to meet or bump together forcefully.

convincing: believable.

counterclockwise: a direction that is the reverse of the way the hands of a clock move.

dazed: unable to think, feel, or move; stunned.

desperate: helpless or acting recklessly due to a loss of hope in a situation that seems impossible to deal with or dangerous in some way.

diagonally: in a slanting direction.

exaggerate: to increase or enlarge beyond what is normal and believable.

extend: to stretch out or straighten to full length.

flex: to move muscles in a way that causes a joint to bend.

flick: (v) to hit or tap with a light, quick stroke in a kind of snapping motion.

flourish: (n) a decorative or showy detail added to make something more attractive.

forearm: the lower part of the arm, from the wrist to the elbow.

horizontal: flat, level, in a side to side position; parallel to the horizon.

impression: a theatrical imitation of a character or situation.

index finger: the first finger of the hand; the finger that is next to the thumb; forefinger.

kazoo: a small plastic or metal, whistlelike instrument with a mouthpiece that adds a buzzing sound to a human voice.

lentils: small, flat seeds that, like peas and beans, grow in a pod and can be eaten.

millet: a type of grain that is grown for foods such as bread and cereal.

prop: (n) an item or object that is not part of the scenery or costumes in a performance for entertainment.

sequence: the order in which one action or event follows another; a series of things.

tilt: (v) to tip or slant something backward, forward, or sideways.

wobble: to move in a clumsy or unsteady way, especially rocking from side to side.

wriggling: twisting and turning from side to side in short, quick motions; squirming.

More Books To Read

The Complete Juggler. Dave Finnegan (Jugglebug)

The Instant Juggling Book. Bob Woodburn (Firefly Books)

Juggling. Hotshots (series). Clive Gifford and Gill Gifford (EDC)

Juggling for All. Colin Francome and Charlie Holland (Players Press)

Juggling for the Complete Klutz. John Cassidy and B.C. Rimbeaux (Klutz, Inc.)

Juggling Step-by-Step. Bobby Besmehn (Sterling)

The Most Excellent Book of How to Be a Juggler. Mitch Mitchelson (Copper Beech Books)

The Ultimate Juggling Kit. Richard Dingman (Running Press/Courage Books)

The Usborne Book of Juggling. How to Make (series). Clive Gifford (EDC)

You Can Juggle. Umbrella Books (series). Peter Murray (Child's World)

Videos

The Complete Teach Yourself to Juggle Video. (Brian Dubé, Inc.)

Juggle Time. Juggling Star. Jugglers Jam. JuggleTime (series). (Jugglebug)

Just Juggle. (Midwest Juggling Co.)

Let's Start Juggling. (MVP Home Entertainment)

The Raspyni Brothers — The Art of Showing Off. (Tapeworm)

You Can Juggle! In Thirty Minutes or Less. (Tapeworm)

Web Sites

www.home.eznet.net/~stevemd/juggle1.html

www.learn2.com/04/0418/0418.php3

Due to the dynamic nature of the Internet, some web sites stay current longer than others. To find additional web sites, use a reliable search engine with one or more of the following keywords: *circus, clowns, jugglers, juggling, magic, Enrico Rastelli*, and *yo-yo*.

Index